i am tired
of being
a dandelion

zane frederick

Printed in the United States of America.

ISBN-13: 978-1975853136

ISBN-10: 197585313X

Edited by Wanda Deglane
Cover art by Laura Supnik
Illustrations by Zane Frederick

to the ones who still wish on expired stars

to the dandelions that have been blown away

to the dreams that will only ever be dreams

i am tired of being a dandelion

zane frederick

i am tired of being a dandelion

overanalyzing

why do i always seem

to read welcome signs

on doors that

remain locked?

the first step

i suppose i do not write to forget you

but rather to remind myself

why i need to

i grab two, just in case

there are not enough

fortune cookies or shooting stars

to reassure me that love

will play out nice for me

iridescent

we rode that bus in silence.

lights flashed after a stop

that wasn't ours and we

glanced at each other three times

before it went dark.

you ran off your stop

in the middle of the

pouring rain.

i always caught your eye

but didn't catch a name.

holding my breath

when you walk by

i'll take my breath away

before you can

how could i risk getting too close

to those lips when we both know

they belong to someone else?

vacancy

fate is a two-way street and i keep drifting

into the other lane, blowing through

the stop signs and every red light.

i must be turning down all the wrong roads.

i must be walking out of the same door empty handed.

the christmas with no gifts

the birthday with no candles

the new year's with no kiss

uncertainty

flush my cheeks and shoot a risk

with a smile from across the room.

leave a napkin with a number

stained with hope and a chance.

waiting is so long for a call

that will never come. head down

with my back against the wall.

i would rather have you say *no*

than to never know at all.

to the blonde host boy

if it is meant to be

it will happen

but i wish it did not

have to take this long

for me to wait and see

if it would become something

that it was never going to be

rapunzel cuts her hair

i never understand why

i plan so far ahead for something

that is not in clear view.

creating fantasies and expectations

of a prince who has not saved me yet.

his horse going in the wrong direction

while i'm trapped in the tower of my mind

waiting for someone to stop by.

empty handed

i'm standing in the middle of a crowded
place and my hands sway in vacancy.
strangers fumble through vinyls and CDs,
stare at my lonely and i can't wait to leave.
see how my friends have found hands to hold
while mine swing patiently
and i imagine, just once, a love that would
reach out for them, or even wait for me.

cupid's bow does not

shoot stars anymore

only eyes i cannot catch

and names that will

never taste my lips

could i have just one more memory?

it is a choice to think about you still.

to have the past packed up in

the attic of my mind, a reminder

that some things will never leave

and i believe storing you in thoughts

may continue to be an excuse to call this *love*

before a new season breezes through my window.

i won't stop looking through old frames

until i find new pictures to put in them.

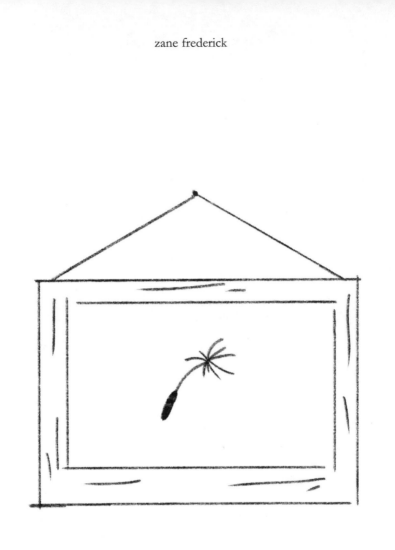

i told you there were too many versions of far away
needed to be put in place so i could move on without
somehow taking you with me.

when people asked about us, or how i was doing,
i swallowed swords. i said i was doing fine when i was far
from it. i said we talk less. spoke of you in the past tense,
as if there was a funeral they had missed. you are more
alive than ever but i have been trying to kill the idea of
you. a big beautiful machete and infatuation to set on fire,
but i forget to mention how you continue to sit criss cross
applesauce inside my pocket. i grab you like car keys

like muscle memory,

like i can't leave without you.

if i were to meet you downtown

i hold on when i shouldn't.

i'll lose circulation

before i ever lose you.

we speak in passing.

in wishing i asked how

your senior year went

and in crosswalks that took us away.

you drift down the alley of people

and i catch up with my friends while

looking back at the crowd.

kauai

was hawaii nice? i should have asked him

because i know that he has never been.

i should have asked about the weather and

if the beaches are warm enough to swim in.

i miss him when i know i'm not supposed to

so i shout it somewhere over the edge.

my tongue is tied in a boy scout knot

to help me swallow what i've never said.

i should have apologized for expecting too much

and for assuming he was drawn to men.

i should have been the first to place some distance

so it wouldn't hurt all of a sudden.

when i moved cities

    to get away from you

        i traveled lightly

           brought my fondest

                moments in a carry-on

                    just enough

                                to get by

you have been

too many

last poems

sleeping hungry

i'm starting to look

like my old self again

but in a body that isn't mine

i continue to sit in the belly of my lonely

as i watch past loves find other mouths to feed

while i gnaw away at the crumbs they left behind

fulfillment

i ache for the pain

of your rejection

i would rather hurt

in all of your noes

than to be buried

in all my alone

that laugh sounded like safety

it was like hearing sirens,

a laugh as loud as an

ambulance when it

flashes in the rearview

mirror of my mind.

i move out of the way

and i hate the way that felt,

watching the laughter

speed away from me

while it goes to save

someone else.

and many more

as each year passes,

i wonder if you will wish me

a happy birthday again.

i wonder how old i will

turn when you stop.

i could receive all

the wishes in the world,

every genie could fill

their lamp up to the brim,

every twisted candle

could burn in my honor

and none of them would

feel as sincere as yours.

i look for your wish in

those bright specks in the sky

when they turn me

twenty at 9:28 p.m.

i wonder if you remember

my birthday anymore.

i wonder if you even

wish me happy.

hibiscus tea in the back room

i visit a place that reeks

of cigarettes and coffee grounds

and your name gets tossed around,

floats amongst heavy conversations

where i pick up the air pockets i hear it in

and i know it's not you, just a different someone

then i leave that place with an after taste of you

on the tip of my tongue

someone has to be honest

just because i want

you to come back

doesn't mean you will

and i probably shouldn't

say this but i can't help

that i think of you still

i am tired of being a dandelion

i have climbed desert mountains

but your lungs still have my breath

what more is there to get over?

what else is left?

1.a.

i'm up

on a rooftop

bar and i'm just ten

months shy of twenty-one

the rum tastes like your bottom lip

and now you've got me coming undone

boy i loved you even then and i love

you even now, all your reckless

and your freckles and

the way you get

me down

TELL ME HOW TO
LOVE SOMEONE NEW
WITHOUT LETTING
GO OF YOU

letting go is overrated

it's singing to their favorite album

until your throat is a rusted trumpet /

it's nights where you take the long way home /

drive past their house to see if the lights are still on /

it's finding an excuse to drag out the hurt

like waiting for them to hang up first /

it's dropping boulders down mountains

or skipping rocks in a lake / sometimes it's

diving in to pick them back up /

it's sprinkling salt in the wound

to make it burn one last time

the last day i saw you was an average one.
summer wind with a handful of stars
on a lit-up backyard where i did not think
you would be and then you were
and my lungs took a break.

they have been holding their breath
for two years now while i keep up with
your life through pictures and stories i
don't want to hear but listen to anyway
because it is all i have left.

that last day is still a wine stain
on all the calendars i hang up.

how dare i long for you.
the earth is tired of spinning
me around the sun and i've lost count
of how many steps we've taken
away from each other.

i let time distance our last conversation
in light years and i still carry the embers
in my mouth when fire falls from the sky.

i burn my tongue calling for you.

when i imagine my first name paired with your last
i pretend it has a ring to it.
i imagine how it will look on christmas cards
and wedding invitations,
how it will taste when i say
it out loud or when i write it
on checks and emails
and thank you letters.
i'll use my favorite pen
and practice my signature,
how to dot the i or
curl the last letter,
how to make it look sweet.

i'll still pretend it sounds right.

and when you're gone

there will be a day when i have nothing left from you.
dusted out of all the basements and cabinets and places
i tried to keep you in. the injuries won't look as familiar
and all the bruises will return to their normal pale hue.
even the pain will grow tired of hurting.

and i'm sure i will drive by sites that used to be ours.
i'm sure they will be covered in new apartment complexes
or patches of grass that grow over our past before i
allowed myself to.

i'm sure i will recall the memories but i won't remember
how they felt. like playing piano for years only to be pulled
away and when you return, you still memorized the
electricity on our fingers skipping the keys. now they just
slow dance, flicking a string to the tune of what used to be

something pretty

i knew from the start you never

liked the same anatomy.

i scraped the apology off my tongue

when i made you out to be the boy

who stayed in all of my reveries,

the face in all my wet dreams and

i'll spend forever apologizing for keeping

you underneath my mind. i'll fold the

words i dropped on your floor nicely,

hang them back in your closet for days

you decide to wear something pretty.

i'm a north star and i keep looking
south for a speck of blue somewhere,
i can almost taste it

someone once said
you were looking for me

most days i hope you still are

in every november

i have pulled muscles letting go

and there's no use missing you in

small talk and when i remember

the daydreams and film scenes

we walked out of together.

i flash back to last days

when my friends said

i deserve better

and i know if i

wait for you

i'll be here

forever.

it's supposed to happen
by chance or fate but
i throw my hands up.
too many what ifs to
talk myself out of,
too many daydreams
have been discontinued,
expired expectations
and outdated wishes
that can no longer be renewed.

winter took me with her crumpled leaves the night i told
you how i felt and when you said you missed me i came
back to tour spring, but all the flowers looked the same

what's the point of hummingbirds migrating
if there is nothing worth coming back for
once the snow stops?

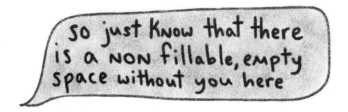

i can't stop you

from leaving but i

can ask you to hold

the door open for me

when you do

infinite

how many hopeless romantics
does it take to build a wall
high enough that keep
our hearts safe?

how many colors need to be
painted until it no longer looks
like your room in golden hour?

how many castles will it take us
to build before we start
believing in happy endings again?

generous

most times i wish we could

talk a little longer

until i pretend to forget why we quit

because i want more

and small talk is insufficient

but with you i'll take what i can get

i will survive

with any love

you provide

the harvest

all my meadows have caught fire and

the wind has stopped exhaling its exhaustion

while i continue to blow dandelions

in your honor or pick off more petals

on flowers because i'll get to say

he loves me

more than once

i don't want him to love me not

self-discipline

i'll tie a string from my bed post

to my hips when the hope starts

floating me up to a universe

where we work out

and i can't promise i won't

cut the string and be left

suspended in mid air

because you make me

want to not come back down

what if he
loves me to
the MOON
but never
on the way
back?

i am tired of being a d

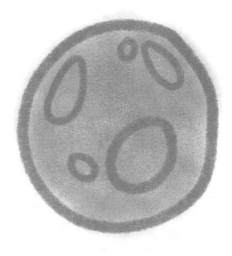

you

go

distances

to

see

me

when they tell you they love you
they will only say it in every way
that isn't what you want it to mean
and it will take everything in you
not to think otherwise.
being so sure of the wrong answer
is a blucprint for the broken.

if they want you then you won't
have to wonder how to make them.

if they love you then you won't have
to die a little each time you try to find proof.

snow in phoenix

arizona feels so lonesome

without you dear

in a heat wave

on this july day

please come back here

rooted

those barbed wires in the garden we grew looked like
flowers i swear. premature carnations and a dandelion
tucked behind my ear. the seeds tickled the idea of
something real stemming from all this. it felt like we never
got enough sun. picked too early from the soil and
dumped in borrowed water that would only last us so
long. i always drank you up when nothing else sufficed.
i anticipated a hundred more rotations together, shoulder
to shoulder. i pictured us back in your neighborhood park
swinging out of rhythm with the gap between our hands,
almost always touching

pittsburgh

and when i love

it's only ever

from far away

never close enough

to stay

wake me up before you leave so i don't have
to see the sunrise before i see you go.

this love is unpredictable and maybe that's the best part.
i sleep by the window and can't tell which direction you
are in, but the iron in my blood drags me south. i haven't
been on that side of you before but maybe i can catch up.
always grazing the skyline searching for blonde hair slicked
back. i keep hitting my head on the atmosphere and i
never know which way i'm facing when you're not around.

where does a balloon go after it floats away?

where do i put my hand after you let it go?

how it ends

some things are never resolved

some questions never answered

what ifs dusted with the past

sometimes closure

is a door left open

why am i so good at ruining good things?
the flowers i bring home give up on me
before i can really breathe them in or place them
in a vase before they get bored.

i forget they still had some growing to do
before i pulled them out of the ground.
picked because i liked their color and their smell
and the way they look in the wind though
never took care of them enough
to make them stick around.

you're not supposed to find the one at nineteen

my father tells me this often
though i am not in search of the one
but rather someone to show me
the paths in a forest i'm not sure
how to get lost in yet

try to learn how to breathe in smoke
before i start the blaze

try to learn how to survive a fire
before i light the match

the hunter lets go

i want to know what it's

like to fall in love again

but i don't want it to

kill me on the way down

i want to chase a butterfly

out of its garden and hope

it stays with me in the wild

but i won't blame it for

going back to where

it came from either

the next one

what if i keep pulling on the fabric of fate

because i'm too afraid to see what becomes of nothing?

i see a train come along but this one doesn't feel right.

to let it pass as i sit for the next one, i don't mind the wait.

i let all these loves walk farther away

since it is safer for them to leave

than it is to stay.

who is going to love someone who turns into

a fire escape when i start smelling smoke?

who turns into an avalanche at a single touch

or a burnt-out lighthouse standing with

my hands rough and hair storm tossed,

knowing a love is coming but i won't let it find me?

someone who can't let good things come into their life

because they leave as quickly as they come.

there are a million things i don't know how to be,

so tell me who is going to love this slow, beating thing?

it's exhausting being cautious

my arms are getting tired of holding up my guard
when you've had daisies in your holster this whole time

i was born with a shotgun laughter and was never one
to aim well at the sky but i will kiss you with the safety off
when you spread your arms out wide, pointing at your lips
saying *hit me where it hurts*

come look

am i doing this right? come look / supervise / i'm trying
to give love / the centaur backs away / i'm holding
candied hearts as bait / come look / why is it so simple
for everyone else? / they sweep feet with grace and cupid
is running out of arrows / i don't think it's in it for me /
not by fate or some made up meant to be / that there is
someone to hold me firm / in all the right places /
to turn my stomach inside out / a feeling that breaks skin
/ i blister before you reach for my hand / come look /
go slow / then go for it

hurt in the hope

i break my fingers while crossing them

and pluck eyelashes off with care,

savoring every wish.

i can't keep losing parts of me

at the expense of a dream

that may not get to exist.

where my father doesn't walk me down the aisle

i have stopped planning for my wedding

when i stopped believing that day would happen.

i carry a bouquet of burnt out daydreams,

slow dance with fear and raise a toast

to all of my lonesome, fading evenings.

no more shooting stars or dragons.

no one on their way to save me.

the rose thorns convince me
that it's safer to be alone
than to be a burden
to someone's
good intentions

every night i walk my lonely home
and before bed i pray that maybe
i won't always be a catastrophe

that maybe i will fall asleep
to two heartbeats
eventually

in the wind
it's there
for a split second,
a whiff of spring
and something real
then it dies off

rust and weight
falling to kiss
the pavement

my knees hurt
from begging and
i'm tired of always
wanting to be saved

i'm an entire forest falling down
but no one turns to hear me.
i can be so much of myself
i think i am too heavy to carry.

i know i'm a lot at once
and something easy to outgrow,
to walk out of in silence
i can hear them tip toe.

i'll start over if i must
with echoes of a new soundtrack.
i swear that i'll fall right off the sidewalk
and promise to never come back.

the bottom

they say there is a light
at the end of the tunnel.
that there is gold at the
bottom of every rainbow
sometimes hope doesn't
come with luck or the sun
it's just wishful thinking.
sometimes there is nothing
at the bottom to discover.

springfield

it's as if i am floating in the still of the unknown

and i don't know how to get to where i want to go.

i seem to miss out on the here and now

by wondering about tomorrow and not knowing how

to be the person i am trying to become.

i'll turn into an entire stormfront,

but where do i start from?

i can't remember if you winked at me

my memories cry rose water on their worst days.

when they can't remember all the tender acts you did

or all the gentle words you said.

you are starting to dry up on my sidewalks

when you used to be a rainstorm

in all my afternoons.

as i pass by

his pupils were telescopes

always pointing down and it's like

i'm floating when i pass by your street,

magic like me only happens

once every so often

i have always been a comet

but you were never looking up

hope

it's the only hand

i've ever been able

to comfortably hold

the hand that never lets go

i am tired of being a dandelion

.

zane frederick

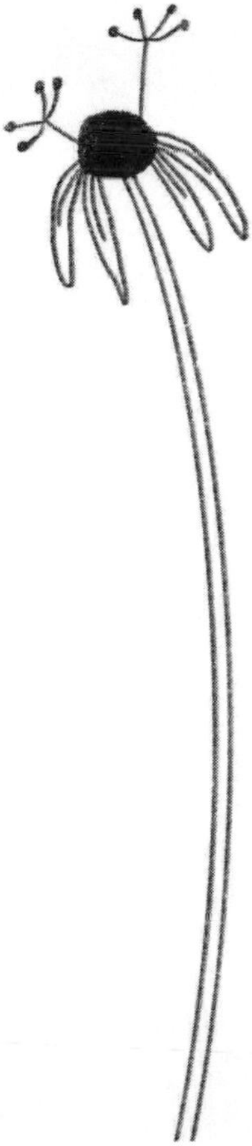

i am tired of being a dandelion

more

if you don't like
the way i love you
then why do you
keep coming back?

serendipity

the pacific sighs when i call out your name

sways her hair over my feet, drags me out

past my ankles and i drop to my knees for the moon

the tides try to stop me from following

the arch of color that hangs above me but

i can't go home without knowing if

you were waiting there at the end

covered in gold

everywhere

there was never a place

where i wasn't yours

parking lots

baseball fields

dance floors

bedrooms

daydreams

i felt like yours

even when i wasn't

when i look at you there are no butterflies
only bees or maybe the feeling of shaking
an etch a sketch after you were done
twisting all my buttons

maybe this is what i've been looking for
when i wasn't paying attention

in the snow

something about the summer makes me more lonely.

how there is more time on my hands left unheld

maybe it's the dry heat that leaves me drained

even when the sun sets.

there's more room in the day to overthink.

it's about the nights that transition into the mornings

i wake up and realize no summer love is

destined for me this june and july.

when august comes i hang

my head on a rack as i search

for winter coats

maybe the snow

will have something for me.

i am afraid to make you laugh and hear

harmonies that lift me high enough to

run my fingers through the milky way

and tell all of jupiter's moons that i might

get to bring you up here with me

silver lining

we have yet to break the edge of small talk
and i still can't figure out what color your eyes are,
too dark to determine. i catch myself leaning in and
i stop before i fall on the verge of your mouth,
one seat away and i don't know how to get closer.

we have yet to have a moment and i'm not sure
how it will sound.
i know how to make us cliché and how to tightrope
across the silver line.
i know how to make you pretty when i write

but i'm still figuring out how to make you mine.

the rush

my stomach is a butterfly garden that has
been closed since the last time there was
a reason for their wings to fly

but i hear the glass start to crack when
our hands get too close for comfort

i'll let this infatuation kill me if it means
i get to break the windows and set them all free

i would even watch it shatter and shimmer if
it meant i got to spin you around as it falls apart

the advent

yesterday i thought about you and it felt
like an honest mistake, human error.
i fold my hands like grandmother taught me and
recite a prayer insincerely, she forgives me.

today i thought about you and it felt like a betrayal,
like the eighth deadly sin. like all the churches closed
on sundays and i got cut on a stained-glass promise that
only bleeds a little but never stops.

tomorrow i will probably think about you and it will
feel like a new religion.
an archangel dressed in black and good intentions.
an almost old testament of a love
that might be born again

in dreams

i still like to write about people i know

i should not be writing about

i know that i want to dream about the space above

and between us with the lights on

but i don't want to have nightmares about

falling off the stratosphere

i don't want to miss you the way i call my mother

after i've stopped breathing

i want to die before everyone else i love

i want to try and save the earth

i want to smoke a cigarette for the placebo effect

i don't want to think about my mother when i do it

i want to believe in happy endings again

i don't want to remember ruined castles

i don't want to keep holding your spot in line

or checking the time and tapping my foot to the sound

of my heart cracking whenever i think you're on your way

8:10 a.m.

i still shoot my shot into space and hope for the best.

i've fallen victim to sunburns and lightning that struck

too close to my feet so i hope the sky is kinder when

i beg her to give me sun, especially in the mornings

when i look in your direction, a strip of green lights and

i'm not afraid to speed up i just

hope you never try to stop me.

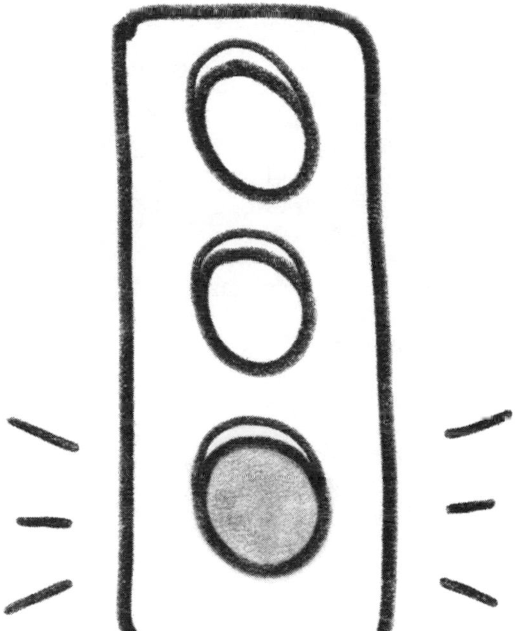

onomatopoeia

small talk will crawl out of my mouth

on days when it looks like

you're about to say something

on days when you forget to take

one more look at me for the road

on days when you choose the seat next to me

only because you are closer to the door

i am tired of being a dandelion

and trying to get you to blow me away

our forte

i'll end up falling for you like snow,

slow and expected. you'll catch me

with your tongue and say my name

out loud for the first time and it will

sound like an orchestra with

more brass, more woodwinds,

more string and percussion.

it will feel like playing with fire,

knowing it will hurt but worth it

enough to find out how bad

above

you look at me like i'm something

NASA is testing in the sky,

like i can both be beautiful and damned,

shiny and too far away to interpret.

like you would be willing to watch

me chase my dreams to jupiter

or crash down to earth when i don't

believe in myself enough to hold

my breath up there.

you look at me like you would

take me in any way that i came

like you aren't afraid to catch a comet

with your bare hands

you are almost at the door

but turn around

to look once more

i am a shooting star

that you cannot ignore

when he said my hips are his favorite

you bore fruit when you leaned in / clementine lips
sprinkled citrus in all my wounds / it stung but the burn
made it feel all the more real / said my hips are pumice /
light in the right places and easy to spin around / surprised
you like my thin / that even my small still fills your hands
when you reach out / feel the nervous and newly wrapped
canvas but you like me in white / the virgin dressed in
innocence with plenty of introverted nights / and once the
stage lights dimmed i opened up like your bedside novel /
my mouth was once a library and you used to whisper
when you entered / then you tore down all the shelves
and turned me into an amphitheater and now you never
fail to make me sing

you walk in the room

and all my guards fall down

i'm a wind chime

and you're a tornado without warning

coming to spin me around

lifetime of poetry

you gave me more in a september than

what i get on christmas day.

gave me enough hope to last me this far

and now i realize how you did just enough damage

so now i always have something to write about.

princess has arrived

i can't decide which one of us was in distress,
it's like we both needed some kind of saving.
i thought love was supposed to be wind in hair
and taste like summer did when we were children,
but each time i leave it only makes the tower ache
for something to hold onto for one more forever.

you can't make a happy ending out of something
that only knows how to fall apart when it's over.

but if midnight keeps looking around and
the horses keep going wild trying to
figure out where all that longing is
coming from, just call out my name
and i'll be coming again.

i like it when i meet
you in my dreams,
it's the only place now
where you don't leave

in these dreams you are so ideal
playing in a field that nobody knows of
and i think we could have been real
if you had just simply shown up

we softly grin from far away
i bite at the nervous under my nails
but this time i don't ask you to stay
and i don't miss you when you're gone

you see i love it when
i meet you in my dreams
now i always get to be
the first to leave

some days i promise that this isn't hopeless

sometimes i say that i'm not still breaking

some days i wait for the door to open

sometimes i promise i'm not waiting

i knew i would see you again

there you are all handsome

hair sticking up, never brushed,

and there i stand all in awe

cotton mouth and blank thoughts

words unable to string together

and hang up a sentence of confession,

how after these empty years

you're still invited to all my parties

the ones with christmas lights

in obscure months and confetti

strewn all over the hardwood floors

and we would tiptoe to your room

lock the door with keys and hands

and finally touch after holding back,

swaddle you in arms that never

grew tired of holding your absence

you are all my daydreams and

i'm afraid that you will know

so give me something to hold onto

when you're letting go

before the band plays

when the crowd walks in, all face paint and confetti
with prideful alma maters and bent trombones,
i am still looking for you despite the noise.
i observe every face and tear the room apart
trying to find something that i always feel like i'm losing.
the room turned into an aquarium and everything was
floating and floating and when i found your laugh before
the drum line started up again it was as though the world
was holding its breath, like it never wanted to continue
spinning until you found my curious, desperate eyes.
some days i wonder if you are still looking
and i can't tell if the world has started
rotating again without waiting for you
to find me

a hundred wishbones
break at my hands
and hold every wish

we're by the door and
i almost taste your chapstick
but no goodbye kiss

and this time you
won't be someone
i learn how to miss

so if you go
then i am
coming with

baby, navy, and even midnight

i'll know i'm over you when

i stop wincing at blue.

when the sky and manhattan beach

don't swallow me in remembrance

of the only shade that feels like a breeze.

i'll know it has passed when i

stop looking for it in specks from afar.

i'll know it most especially

the day i forget what color

your eyes are.

i danced through my seventeenth summer as i slowly
slipped into the autumn of his life / covered in earlier
sunsets and passionfruit tea / he left me in a winter that
lasted too long / watched him bloom in the remaining
seasons of what could have been our first spring and every
summer after that / though we never made it that far /

had to grow new thorns and petals / learned how to dance
again / bare feet in the grass / cherishing this june /
drinking up her laugh / and all of her weekends

they tell me not to touch this kind of love

that it is dancing through rose thorns

and right below lightning storms

but i'll meet it in car conversations

and pin dropped locations

even if hearts

don't end up

collided

i think it's still love

even if it's unrequited

if it wasn't love

then why did it

feel like it was?

go ahead and break my hands if it means

i'll stop planting what ifs at your feet and

checking them every morning to see

if they grew at all overnight

even the slightest bit

the second time

i've never nose-dived out of the sky

but i know what it feels like when i fall asleep

i don't know what it's like to be called beautiful

but i know how to say it to myself and mean it

i haven't figured out how to stop myself from falling

but i'm glad to have tasted the courage to jump

the blue in your eyes aren't as light as his

but i know how to float in them still

i'm not sure if this is how love is supposed to look

but at least it feels like it

my heart is cracking beneath

your footsteps and i learned

ballet to the sound of its pieces

floating away

in the distance

i'm told you will find it when you're least expecting,

when you're walking with your eyes closed

and arms crossed,

but how do i stop myself from looking?

my father reminds me of my age,

how i am just beginning my roaring twenties

and that there will be other cheeks to kiss

and more eyes to miss

so why waste my time searching for something

i cannot predict?

i keep finding three leaf clovers in my pockets

i keep watching planes fly to see where

they're going to land

i keep crossing the street and checking both ways

things to be hopeful for

(with confidence, with caution)

for tomorrow, and tomorrow's tomorrow

that my father's eyes will never dry out

for my mother to feel twenty-one when she's fifty-one

that i will get to where i have been trying to go

for sea turtles to make it to the other side of the ocean

that air won't run out and it will still taste good

for the oceans to be free of plastic and human error

that people will stop smoking cigarettes

that people will start paying attention

that you will come back

that i will come back

what are you hopeful for?

(with confidence, with caution)

_____

_____

_____

_____

_____

_____

_____

_____

_____

_____

it's been four years and
i'm still letting go

so it might take a thousand
more tomorrows

before i move on
for the hundredth time

but for now i'll let you
live free in my mind

maybe you forgot when i told you everything.
when you asked for space on your birthday but
i gave you the world instead and on the off days
i handed you the rest of the solar system and research
invested into finding something more infinite
than what i see when you look at me.
i dip my hands into black holes like empty pockets
searching for loose change and sunflower seeds to
pull out as a peace offering or a shot in the dark.

maybe you will go and plant something i have
been trying to water for years now.
maybe something will bud if you
believe in it for once.

because you were the first

yes

even now

even when i shouldn't

yes out loud and

in hallway whispers

yes in the dark

and in public spaces

yes in therapy

and blurry faces

yes in every lifetime

where we could've worked

yes on picked petals

and loose eyelashes

yes

even when it hurts

a. yes

b. always

c. a & b

blonder days

my thoughts set up a blanket
in a park we swung in / i fall
again, like autumn leaves before
winter comes and takes it all
away from me / the day feels warm /
golden hour lasts longer than usual /
memories loop around the acre and
laughter whistles in the wind that
took the candle's flame before you
made a wish / i say a bad joke and
all i remember are your dancing,
swirling eyes

forgetting

just because they

still live in your mind

tucked behind memories

and places they made room in

does not mean you haven't moved on

it just means they stayed long enough

to carve initials under parts you can't see

you are allowed to mourn their absence

without wishing for their return

i misplace my grace

each time i see your lovely face

but these clouds turn gray

when i look your way

so perhaps it's time

to consider myself

and start chasing dreams

instead of someone else

that's it
i'm putting the sun in every corner so that it
starts to hurt when i look up

i'm pulling the tides up and over the x in the sand
so i stop believing i can find you easily

i'm staring straight ahead while crossing the road so i don't
keep looking both ways for someone that isn't coming

i'm stomping on every dandelion so that i never
give another wish to summer's tongue

i'll close my eyes when someone starts shooting
pretty stars so i can stop chasing things that fall
further away from me

i am capsizing under you
but i am not sinking

this love is pulling me in
but i am not falling

i am doing this slowly and
with calculated movements

i am not this flickering spark
but i am the ballerina
i dreamed to become
the first time i even
thought about dancing
for someone other
than myself

therapy on 7th

who are all these sad songs i listen to for?

i used to curl into the holes of cellos

and warped wood violins

but now i dance inside of flutes

and sounds of 80s synth

the bar on 7th is telling me how to be alive

with catchy melodies and another sad song

by kelly clarkson singing about how to breathe

for the first time since you've been gone

who were all those i used to miss?

not one name comes to mind

not even his

buried

i believe i am still recovering

i'm under the rubble and have stopped screaming,

been so used to having something

on top of me at all times

that my voice has forgotten how to ask for help

how do you become something that

grows in between the cracks?

some days i can almost hear sirens in the distance

i have to believe someone will save me eventually

learning to love this body

was like trying to push

through season one

before the show got good

it was waiting for

the dough to rise

for the sun to set

for a new year's eve countdown

it was being my own

best friend long enough

to understand how much

i deserve a love story too

white dress
most nights
i am dressed
as the moon,
half empty
half full,
but some nights
i am all whole,
complete,
bright enough
to blind those
who thought
less of me,
big enough
to keep the sun
in hiding

bigger

i used to tuck my knees in
on the plane ride home.
try not to take up as much space.
became an airplane bathroom
all tight and cramped
and nowhere else to go

but my knees felt the growing pains.

now i spread my legs when i sleep.
take up two seats on the bus.
make chairs push themselves in
as i walk through recklessly.
i don't need to fit anywhere.

i'll take up space in this
whole god damn place.

being kind to myself

was a forgotten art,

learned to drag my

yesterdays by the wrist,

such a heavy reminder

not of where i once was

but where i am still going

on track

i have to trust this universe

has some sort of plan for me,

that all these misguided moments

are supposed to put me on

the right track for the right things.

that this ferris wheel of hope

will one day bring me up to see

the view of something i never

even thought existed at all.

now i sleep in

on days you come in loud

so early morning construction,

i do my best to block out the sound

from the nights you stretched out

that ruined every one of my mornings

but now i thankfully remember

how to live my life on days you're not around

i've gone to bigger cities
been swallowed by an even
bigger mouth
i know how to hide in the dark
but this lonely is not as cold as
people say it's supposed to be

sometimes it's a blanket fort
or a bomb shelter
it's safe and warm
and there are flowers in every corner
that do not die when i wake up

turning twenty

the candle wax melts onto my cake as i look back

at the city i set on fire

aspirations and checklists i set aside for tomorrow

only to never complete them

i blow out my candles and walk back to the ashes

with hopes to build a new resolution where i do the things

i said i would do yesterday

i'll repaint the city gold

i'll turn on all the lights

to think about you still is a sin with no harm
it feels like a blessing but doesn't make it right,
when you wave in the backdrop of my dreams
i whisper your name out of my own spite

and if i had any self-control i would
return to every wild, infinite night
but you already took me to the sun
and i don't need to go there twice

my therapist told me to fly

the winter in me felt infinite,

but now i am the fox after hibernation

the birds that return from the south,

the city of seattle under the sun.

warmth graced my skin like

it has been looking for me.

the tiny hairs across my limbs

stand tall, stretch out their bodies,

i think they feel it too.

what if #1,118

there has to be a universe somewhere out there in which
we make it, where we end up in the way i always wrote
about but not all good things happen how they are
supposed to

there are hundreds of lifetimes where i could have decided
differently. where i could have just gone home instead of
taking you with me. or where i didn't ask you to a dance or
learn that song on piano. or where i didn't keep saying yes
despite having every reason not to

even in all those multiverses where good things happen,
i know we still wouldn't have made it out hand in hand

no amount of what ifs can change back stars
from exploding and reigniting
you can't make someone fall in love with you
no matter how many times you dream
of doing yesterday differently

to do list for the lonely

make a dinner reservation under your name, table for one

order two glasses of wine then the whole damn bottle

be the loudest person screaming during the scary movie

clap when the plane lands for the cliché of being alive

revisit the crosswalk where he went to the north pole

run to the south pole so that you are the first to move on

learn to swim in the deep end of the pool
    (let your head go under once)

hum to the floorboards when the lonely gets too heavy

laminate each promise and don't let them touch the floor

remember every sad day is a monument to some place
much happier

i keep my eyes closed

i'm sorry

you're not yet invited

inside my mind

because i'm a lot

but maybe

you'll like it

how the scars healed

i hide behind books and the fear of being known again,

having to repeat my favorite things,

show you the wounds just to explain

why my hands look the way they do,

why i kiss with hesitation,

why i tell you to take it slow,

and why i close my eyes

when we pass by certain streets

perhaps we learn

to love the lonely

even when we think

no one else will

to sit in silence

on our long days

to bathe in solidarity

shut our eyes and smile

as we put our head under

the luxury of solidarity

what a life to live

to have not known love

referred to as singular pronouns

but never as *us*

at times i'm afraid to regret

the almosts

and the weight of

what could have been

though i bask in

peace and relief

of a romance

that never happened

i'm a disco ball spinning in a room
full of slow dancers and corsages,
first times and high heels lined up
against the wall waiting to be claimed.
i sparkle in every light and rotate at my
own pace to whatever song is playing.
the slow dancers are blended together,
barely breathing, just leaning into
chests and shoulders but i am
still sparkling, still spinning,
even when the lights go out.

when the dancing is across the room and you are still a
wallflower that only sways without being noticed / know
that you are greater than anyone who makes you feel small
/ that you are a walking spotlight in an empty auditorium
but there are people still cheering for you somewhere /
and others who have yet to see your grace will someday
/ i hope you never stop dancing on your own

out of the blue

don't plan for love that hasn't come

they're on their way

the quiet days and all the pain

are worth the wait

they will come and you will fall

right into place

and when love says they're here to stay

they won't hesitate

it's brave to be lost

we are asked who we want to be

when we grow up and you can

hear every captive breath

the humming hesitation

the doubt

you can still grow into

the person you wish to be

without waiting to grow up

or rushing too quickly

it's okay if your futures

don't yet have a horizon

to live life in pitch black

but those days will brighten

wait and see

the sky will turn upside down

and alaska will break off from

her right-hand man before i ever stop

wondering if you're happy where you are.

your eyes close as the sun hides behind earth

and you probably never want to wake up.

your lungs are still looking for a way to breathe

for better reasons than just simply surviving.

your life is full of fruit and memories that have

spoiled but have you thought about the ones

covered in sugar you have yet to live through?

look up
there could be
a storm on the way
that you cannot see
coming
nor know how
to run from

but you can still
look up and at least take
in the sky and her sun
while you still have it

love lights

i build myself a safe house that never hurts me

but i keep staring out the window and looking out

at all the love lights in the distance

all that wild freedom

the rib rubbed laughter

the deliberate kisses

with hands that don't let go

and if i were brave enough i would run to the lights too

ride the carousel and hold on for dear life

sometimes i open the door to hear the music

i may even step out on the porch

just to see the lights glisten

by 2030

before the universe breaks apart

i'll find a face that looks

better moonlit than sun kissed,

i'll be given the space it takes

for two people to fall safe,

and that face will keep the promises

you used to break

the ones that never got enough daylight

the ones you couldn't save

i think about how it doesn't hurt anymore.
how i only talk to you when it's your birthday.
how it seems that i've started to age like whiskey,
a slow, sweet burn.

i think about how much longer your hair got.
i think about you putting your hand on top
of mine while i reached for quarters to buy us coffee.

i think about how sweet i used to make my coffee.
i think about the way i asked if you felt the same,

the way you said *no*.

i think about the distance.
how long it took
to stop associating places with people.
how to order coffee hot instead of iced,
how to take it black and bitter.

i think about the notes and notions i left in a box.
i think about how i don't think of you.

sprouting

i stepped all over my gardens

to keep up with my mistakes,

to hold on to you without having to ask

and pleasing all those who never

earned the daisies i grew.

now there are thorns in

places that used to be softest

and holes in the ground where

i tried to bury myself breathing.

yesterday i found seeds in my pockets

and glove compartment

and behind my back teeth.

i will grow new gardens

once the sun comes back

and i tell her i won't leave

them to die this time.

convergence

the sky let down her hair and you climbed up to saturn.
walked in circles around her rings then placed one on your
finger.

when you were ready to go, you leaped, floated slow and
gracefully. crashed down to earth arriving so dangerously
and extraordinarily without fault or error onto the asphalt
i rode training wheels on. ran in circles in search of the life
that will fit in your gravity.

you'll find me in a parked car on top of an arizona
mountain and it won't feel like toronto or saturn's rings.
not even a san francisco breeze but perhaps
a new beginning

if i am to find a love
so refreshing my father's
shoulders drop in relief,
the darling my mother
pictured me safe with,
the angel that all of
my friends root for,
the one that makes
me the kind of happy
i told my therapist
i wanted to be,
the love that i
kept writing about

the uranometria at grand central station

i'm waiting the way i wait for spring and then summer,
for all of my tears to turn to mist

i'm waiting for a lifetime in which i do not write myself
into somebody else's world, they pen me first

i'm waiting for the 6 train in the middle of my life
to take me uptown or anywhere as long as i'm going up

i'm waiting for love like a carnation looking for sun
but blooming is not an overnight miracle

i'm waiting for traffic lights to turn green
so that i can keep moving on

i don't know where i'm going
but at least i'm on my way

i am tired of being a dandelion

i am tired of being a dandelion

acknowledgments

a special thank you to Laura Supnik for illustrating the cover and making this book come to life.

an immense thank you to all my friends and family who have rooted for me throughout this entire process. i would not have the confidence to release this without their love.

thank you to my readers who have stuck by me and waited patiently for this collection. the support means everything.

to the loves that inspired these works. thank you for not falling for me. thank you for saying *no*. thank you for saying *yes*. thank you for choosing someone else.

to the magazines that have previously published the following:
"come look" (page 70)
    – The Tunnels
"i knew i would see you again" (page 108)
    – The Tunnels
"uncertainty" (page 14)
    – Milk + Beans
"in the snow" (page 90)
    – Mohave He[art] Review
"that laugh sounded like safety" (page 29)
    – Pulp Poets Press
"and many more" (page 30)
    – Soft Cartel

thank you forever,

zane

i am tired of being a dandelion

Zane Frederick is a writer from Phoenix, Arizona. He first started writing in the fourth grade but really picked up the hobby in his early high school days. Zane is still writing, still being the best version of himself possible. He self-published his debut poetry collection, (he)art., in 2018.

Contact & stay connected with him:

Instagram: @zanefrederickwrites

Email: zanefrederickwrites@gmail.com